HOW   PE

BISON

IN AMERICAN HISTORY

NORMAN D. GRAUBART

PowerKiDS press™

New York

Published in 2015 by The Rosen Publishing Group, Inc.
29 East 21st Street, New York, NY 10010

First Edition

Editor: Amelie von Zumbusch
Photo Research: Katie Stryker
Book Design: Colleen Bialecki

Photo Credits: Cover, pp. 15, 17, 18 MPI/Stringer/Archive Photos/Getty Images; p. 5 Purestock/Thinkstock; p. 6 centrill/iStock/Thinkstock; p. 8 Top Photo Corporation/Top Photo Group/Thinkstock; p. 9 Jason Rowland/ iStock/Thinkstock; p. 10 DEA Picture Library/De Agostini Picture Library/Getty Images; p. 11 George Catlin/The Bridgeman Art Library/Getty Images; p. 12 National Archives at College Park/U.S. National Archives and Records Administration; p. 13 (top) Zack Frank/Shutterstock.com; p. 13 (bottom) Shane Maritch/Shutterstock.com; p. 14 Rick Rudnicki/Lonely Planet Images/Getty Images; p. 19 photo-trip/iStock/Thinkstock; p. 20 Bob Thomas/Popperfoto/Getty Images; p. 21 gqxue/iStock/Thinkstock; p. 30 McKinneMike/iStock/Thinkstock.

Library of Congress Cataloging-in-Publication Data

Graubart, Norman D.
 Bison in American history / by Norman D. Graubart. — First edition.
    pages cm. — (How animals shaped history)
Includes index.
 ISBN 978-1-4777-6757-3 (library binding) — ISBN 978-1-4777-6758-0 (pbk.) —
ISBN 978-1-4777-6626-2 (6-pack)
 1. American bison—History—Juvenile literature. 2. West (U.S.)—History—Juvenile literature. I. Title.
 QL737.U53G76 2015
 599.64'3—dc23
                                                        2013046666

Manufactured in the United States of America

CPSIA Compliance Information: Batch # WS14PK5: For Further Information contact Rosen Publishing, New York, New York at 1-800-237-9932

CONTENTS

MEET THE BISON

There are two main species of bison, the American bison and the European bison. American bison are sometimes called buffalo. For thousands of years, people have hunted bison for their **hides** and their meat.

Before the nineteenth century, there were millions of bison all over North America. There may have been more than 30 million bison in the Great Plains region alone. Bison are one of the symbols of North America. They appear on the buffalo nickel coin, the Wyoming state flag, and even the logo for the National Football League team the Buffalo Bills, which are based in Buffalo, New York.

Bison are North America's largest land animal. Their thick brown fur is usually longer and darker around their heads.

ABOUT BISON

Bison are **mammals**. They are closely related to cows. Their eyesight is not very good, but they have excellent senses of hearing and smell. Bison are **herbivores**. This means they eat only plants. Their main food is grass.

Bison have thick, woolly hair, tough skin, and horns. They are slightly taller than human beings but much heavier. They can weigh more than 2,000 pounds (907 kg).

Bison can run as fast as 35 miles per hour (56 km/h).

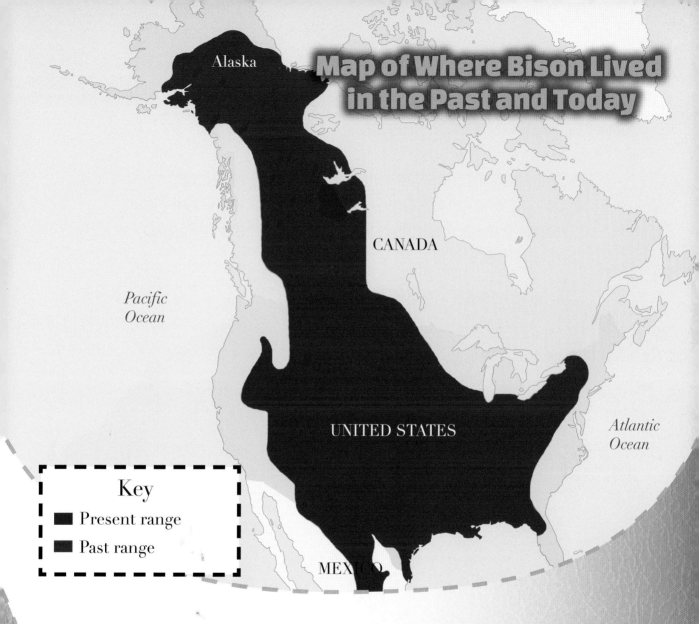

Alaska

CANADA

Pacific Ocean

UNITED STATES

Atlantic Ocean

MEXICO

Key
Present range
Past range

American bison can be found as far south as the US-Mexico border and as far north as Alaska. However, there are only about 20,000 bison scattered over this large range.

SHAPING THE PLAINS

American bison live in small herds along the Rocky Mountains and on the Great Plains. Much of the Great Plains is **prairie**. Prairie habitats have large, open fields of grass, warm summers, and cold winters.

Bison are always on the move, looking for fresh grass to eat. They cover big distances as they roam.

This bison is wallowing. Wallowing bison created some buffalo wallows and made others larger.

Bison help shape the prairie **ecosystem**. Buffalo like to roll around in dirt patches called buffalo wallows. Buffalo wallows allow water to pool in otherwise flat areas. This can help keep the soil wet. Also, bison spread seeds as they eat grass and move around. Bison usually eat the dominant, or most common, kinds of grass. This leads to a wider variety of grasses on the plains.

Bison were important to the Native Americans of the Great Plains. Plains tribes such as the Comanches, Crows, and Apaches used every part of the bison. Because of this, some people who study Native Americans call the bison the Plains Indians' supermarket.

This painting shows members of the Sioux tribe hunting bison in the nineteenth century. As you can see, they used snowshoes and dog sleds to hunt in the snow.

This print from the 1830s shows Native American hunters dressed in wolf skins sneaking up on bison. This trick worked because wolves almost never attack bison in herds and bison know this.

Native American men often hunted bison with arrows. After the Spanish brought horses to North America, Plains tribes hunted on horseback. If they needed more buffalo, they did something else. A few men would surround a herd of bison, run at them, and force them to jump over a cliff. The cliffs used for this are known as buffalo jumps.

TIMELINE

1833

American bison are already **extinct** in lands east of the Mississippi River.

1872

Yellowstone National Park becomes the first American national park.

1800   1810   1820   1830   1840   1850   1860

1803

President Thomas Jefferson buys the territory of Louisiana from France for $3 million. This includes nearly all of the Great Plains.

1875

General Philip Sheridan suggests that Congress do nothing to stop buffalo hunting so that Native Americans will be driven off their lands.

1928

Bison from Montana are brought to Alaska, where they still live today.

| 1870 | 1880 | 1890 | 1900 | 1910 | 1920 | 1930 |

1900

Congress passes the Lacey Act, making it illegal to sell an animal if it has been killed illegally, even in another state. This makes it harder for hunters to sell bison.

1913

The first buffalo nickel is minted.

13

You may think that Native Americans hunted bison just for food. They did eat buffalo meat. In fact, the tongue was considered the tastiest part by many tribes! However, Indians hunted bison for all their body parts. They would use hair to stuff pillowcases, the hide to make moccasins, and the horns for containers and arrow points. The **bladder** was used to make medicine bags. They even used bison fat to make paint!

Several Native American tribes dried bison meat over fires like this one to make pemmican. This preserved food is made from dried meat and melted fat. It often includes berries.

This bison robe was made by members of the Hidatsa tribe. Men of the Plains tribes painted robes with figures on them, while women made ones with geometric designs.

Usually, the men did the hunting. The women did the hard work of cleaning the hides, shaving the hair, and making items from the rest of the parts.

15

HEAVY HUNTING

In the early years of the United States, European Americans began to use bison hides for winter coats. As Americans moved west, where bison were more common, they **traded** with Native Americans for bison hides. Native Americans usually did the work of hunting the bison and preparing its hide and fur.

As more Americans moved to the Midwest and West, they began to hunt bison on their own. Often, they hunted bison for their meat. Other times, they did it for sport. These hunters killed huge numbers of bison. By 1890, there were only around 1,000 bison in all of North America.

American hunters killed millions of bison. Many were killed for their hides. In the winter of 1872 to 1873 alone, hunters shipped 1.5 million bison hides east.

GONE WITH THE BISON

During the centuries before American settlers arrived, many Plains tribes had been **nomadic**. This meant that they moved around with the bison to hunt them. Throughout the nineteenth century, the American government forced tribes onto smaller and smaller pieces of land. This meant they could no longer travel with bison herds.

Native Americans often moved loads from place to place with a travois. This had two poles with a platform, net, or buffalo hide between them. It was pulled by a horse or dog.

By 1880, most of the bison on the Great Plains had been killed off.

Americans also hunted the bison nearly to extinction. Because bison were so important to Plains tribes, many of the Native Americans who depended on them died or were **displaced**. The US government knew this would happen. They were fighting with Native Americans for territory, so they did nothing to stop hunters from killing bison.

SAVING THE BISON

The US government began to view the near extinction of the bison as a problem. Bison had become a symbol of North America. Also, **conservationists** began to learn what dangers extinction could mean for the whole region. President Theodore Roosevelt began setting aside large areas of western land to protect the environment. This helped save the bison!

In 1905, Theodore Roosevelt helped form the American Bison Society to protect and restore bison. Like many early conservationists, Roosevelt was a hunter.

Yellowstone National Park is the only place in the United States where bison have lived continuously. All other US populations had to be reintroduced to their areas.

Zoos became important in bison conservation. The Bronx Zoo, in New York City, brought 15 bison to Oklahoma to roam the prairie in 1907. Ranchers began raising bison to sell their meat. This increased the overall bison **population**, too.

North America's bison were saved because people began to worry about their extinction. Today, it is legal to hunt buffalo, but the hunting is very highly **regulated**. This means that there are a lot of rules about how, where, and when they can be hunted.

Hunting is a good sign for the future. It means that the population is coming back, and one of America's great symbols will continue to graze the Great Plains.

The bison that live in the United States are either raised by ranchers or are part of publicly owned herds.

GLOSSARY

bladder (BLA-der) The part of the body that stores urine.

conservationists (kon-ser-VAY-shun-ists) People who want to protect nature.

displaced (dis-PLAYSD) Pushed out of a place.

ecosystem (EE-koh-sis-tem) A community of living things and the surroundings in which they live.

extinct (ik-STINGKT) No longer existing.

herbivores (ER-buh-vorz) Animals that eat only plants.

hides (HYDZ) The skins of animals.

mammals (MA-mulz) Warm-blooded animals that have backbones and hair, breathe air, and feed milk to their young.

nomadic (noh-MA-dik) Roaming about from place to place.

population (pop-yoo-LAY-shun) A group of animals or people living in the same place.

prairie (PRER-ee) A large place with flat land and grass but few or no trees.

regulated (REH-gyoo-layt-ed) Controlled.

traded (TRAYD-ed) Bought or sold goods.

INDEX

A
Americans, 16, 19

C
conservationists, 20
cows, 6

E
ecosystem, 9
eyesight, 6

F
food, 6, 14

H
hearing, 6
herbivores, 6

hide(s), 4,
  14–16
hunting, 12,
  15–16, 22

L
land(s), 12, 18, 20

M
mammals, 6
meat, 4, 14, 16

N
Native Americans, 10,
  12, 14, 16, 19
North America, 4, 11,
  16, 20, 22

P
plants, 6
population, 21, 22
prairie, 8, 21

R
region, 4, 20

S
senses, 6
settlers, 18
species, 4
symbol(s), 4, 20, 22

T
tribes, 10–11, 14,
  18–19

WEBSITES

Due to the changing nature of Internet links, PowerKids Press
has developed an online list of websites related to the subject
of this book. This site is updated regularly. Please use this link
to access the list:

www.powerkidslinks.com/anhi/bison/